ok is to be returned on or before
he last date sta   d below.

Wild World

Watching Cobras in Asia

Louise and Richard Spilsbury

Heinemann
LIBRARY

www.heinemann.co.uk/library

Visit our website to find out more information about Heinemann Library books.

To order:

☎   Phone 44 (0) 1865 888066

▤   Send a fax to 44 (0) 1865 314091

▱   Visit the Heinemann Bookshop at www.heinemann.co.uk/library to brows our catalogue and order online.

First published in Great Britain by Heinemann Library, Halley Court, Jordan Hill, Oxford OX2 8EJ, part of Harcourt Education. Heinemann is a registered trademark of Harcourt Education Ltd.

Editorial: Nancy Dickmann and Sarah Chappelow
Design: Ron Kamen and edesign
Illustrations: Martin Sanders
Picture Research: Maria Joannou and Christine Martin
Production: Camilla Crask
Originated by Modern Age
Printed and bound in Italy by Printer Trento srl

ISBN 0 431 19066 6
10 09 08 07 06
10 9 8 7 6 5 4 3 2 1

British Library Cataloguing in Publication Data
Spilsbury, Louise and Richard
Watching cobras in Asia. – (Wild world)
597.9'64217'095
A full catalogue record for this book is available from the British Library.

Acknowledgements
The Publishers would like to thank the following for permission to reproduce the following photographs: Alamy Images pp. 17 (Bruce Coleman), 18 (Bruce Coleman), 27 (Mervyn Rees); ANT Photo Library p. 20 (John Weigel); Ardea pp. 22 (Adrian Warren), 28 (Steve Downer); Corbis pp. 7 (Ric Ergenbright), 9 (Joe McDonald); Ecoscene p. 16 (Photocyclops); Getty Images pp. 5 (Digital Vision), 8 (PhotoDisc), 11 (PhotoDisc, 24 (ImageBank); National Geographic Image Collection pp. 10 (Mattias Klum), 12 (Mattias Klum); Nature PL pp.15 (Ashok Jain), 23 (Mary McDonald), 26 (John Downer); NHPA pp. 4 (Daniel Heuclin), 13 (Daniel Heuclin), 14 (Daniel Heuclin), 21 (Daniel Heuclin); Rex Features pp. 19, 25. Cover photograph of a cobra reproduced with permission of Science Photo Library/Peter B. Kaplan.

The publishers would like to thank Michael Bright of the BBC Natural History Unit for his assistance in the preparation of this book.

Every effort has been made to contact copyright holders of any material reproduced in this book. Any omissions will be rectified in subsequent printings if notice is given to the publishers. The paper used to print this book comes from sustainable resources.

Contents

Meet the cobras 4

The warm places cobras live 6

Spot the cobra! 8

King cobra land 10

Moving around 12

Night hunter 14

Cobra strike 16

Meeting up .18

Cobra nest .20

The first months 22

Cobra warnings 24

Snakes and people 26

Tracker's guide 28

Glossary 30

Find out more 31

Index 32

Words written in bold, **like this**, are explained in the glossary.

Meet the cobras

This is Asia, the home of cobras. Cobras are a kind of snake. All snakes have long thin bodies and no legs. Their skin is covered in tough **scales**.

▸▸ *Watch out for cobras like this in wild places in Asia.*

There are many different kinds of cobra. The biggest kind is the king cobra. All cobras are **venomous**. That means they have poisonous bites.

▲ *This cobra is a spitting cobra. It can spit and bite* **venom.**

The warm places cobras live

Many cobras live in the **continent** of
Asia. King cobras live only in southern
Asia. Some other kinds of cobra live in
the continent of Africa.

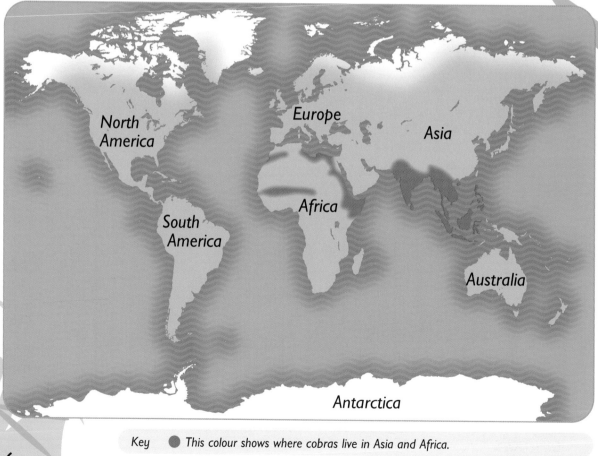

Key   ● This colour shows where cobras live in Asia and Africa.

Southern Asia has a **tropical climate**. There is a long, dry season and a short, wet season. It is always warm, but it is hottest just before the wet season.

▲ *Plants grow fast in a tropical climate. Many animals live amongst the plants.*

Spot the cobra!

A king cobra can be tricky to spot in its **tropical** home. Its skin is a similar colour to the leaves on the forest floor.

▲ *When an animal is a similar colour to the place it lives, we say it is **camouflaged**.*

King cobras can grow to the length of a car! Sometimes a snake's skin becomes worn out. It wriggles out of the old skin. There is a brand new skin underneath.

▲ When a cobra grows out of its ragged old skin, it is called **moulting**.

King cobra land

King cobras live in **tropical rainforests**. A rainforest has lots of tall trees. There is a tangle of smaller plants on the damp ground.

In a rainforest, cobras often lie near streams. This helps them stay cool when it is hot.

This king cobra is moving through tropical grassland.

Some king cobras live in tropical **grasslands**. Here there are lots of tall, dry grasses. On cool mornings, cobras lie out in the sun to get warm.

Moving around

King cobras can move in different ways.
They slither along the ground. They coil
and twist amongst branches.

▲ *King cobras swim well. They bend their bodies*
backwards and forwards to move through water.

Snakes use the big **scales** on their belly to move. When they stretch and shorten their body, the scales grip the ground. This helps them move.

All snakes have wide, thick scales on their bellies.

13

Night hunter

Cobras usually hunt at night. They can see in dim light. When it is completely dark, they can feel animals moving near by.

⬆ *By flicking out its tongue this king cobra picks up smells of other animals.*

Most cobras hunt rats, lizards, and frogs to eat. But the king cobra has a taste for other **tropical** snakes! It quietly moves close enough to bite them.

🔺 Rat snakes are one of the king cobra's favourite **prey**.

Cobra strike

When a king cobra strikes, it jabs two sharp, hollow **fangs** into its **prey**. The cobra squirts **venom** through the fangs. The venom stops the prey breathing.

▶▶ *The king cobra attacks quickly.*

The king cobra opens its mouth wide and swallows the prey whole. Cobra venom helps to **digest** the prey. It breaks the prey down into little pieces of food.

▲ *A big meal will fill a cobra up for several days.*

Meeting up

In the dry season, adult king cobras meet up to **mate**. King cobras usually live alone. They only come together to mate.

⬆ *Females smell different when it is time to mate. Males can follow their scent trail.*

King cobras are rarely seen together in the wild. These two are living in a snake farm.

If two **male** cobras find the same **female**, they will fight each other. The loser slithers away. The winner mates with the female.

Cobra nest

A **female** king cobra makes a leafy nest. She usually lays her eggs before the wet season. Heavy rains could wash the eggs away.

▲ *The female lays up to 40 rubbery eggs in her leaf and soil nest.*

The mother wraps herself around the eggs. This keeps them warm as the baby snakes develop inside. She guards the nest from egg-eating animals.

▲ The female lies coiled on her nest for two months to **incubate** her eggs.

The first months

In the wet season, the baby king cobras hatch from their eggs. Their hungry mother leaves. The babies grow fast. They **moult** once a month.

▲ *Newly-hatched king cobras are the width of your little finger.*

*The bright **scales** on baby king cobras warn other animals that they are **venomous**.*

Baby cobras use their **venom** to catch small **prey** such as frogs. They also use it to defend themselves. Mongooses, ants, and other snakes try to kill baby cobras.

23

Cobra warnings

Adult king cobras have few **predators**. But they do not like other animals to get too close. Cobras warn them off by puffing out their neck to make their head look big.

▶▶ *This king cobra is warning animals it will strike if they get too close.*

A spot on the back of a cobra's head looks like a big eye. This scares some animals off!

The king cobra also makes a warning sound like a dog's growl. If its warnings do not work, the cobra may strike. One bite has enough **venom** to kill an elephant.

Snakes and people

Adult king cobras are quite shy. They usually keep away from people. In Asia the **rainforests** where cobras live are being cut down.

🔺 *When people clear land for farming, wild animals are forced to move elsewhere.*

If king cobras have to move close to villages to find food, people may kill them. The king cobras that survive live on to have their own young in the future.

⏏ *Doctors collect **venom** to make medicine that saves people from cobra bites.*

Tracker's guide

In the wild, king cobras are usually difficult to spot. You have to know how to track them.

*The easiest way to know they are around is by finding old skins. Adult cobras **moult** four times a year.*

Sometimes you can find snake tracks. It
is impossible on the leafy forest floor, but
if you are lucky you might find tracks on
sandy ground.

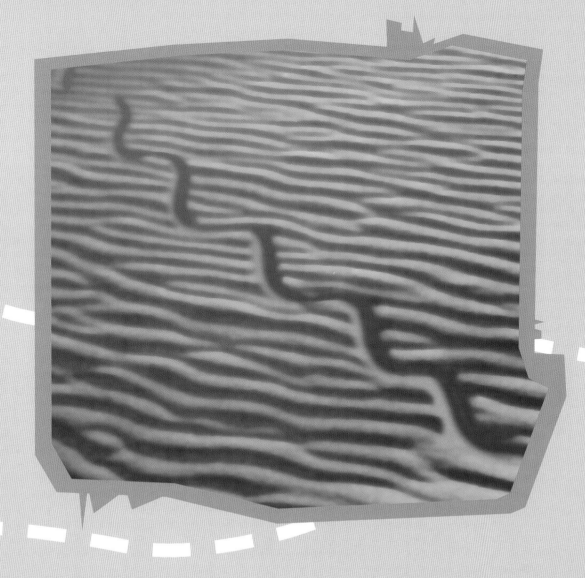

Glossary

camouflage colours and patterns that hide an animal where it lives

climate types of weather a place gets most years

continent the world is split into seven large areas of land called continents. Each continent is divided into different countries.

digest break down food inside an animal's body

fang sharp, pointed front tooth

female animal that can become a mother when it grows up. Women and girls are female people.

grassland area of land mainly covered in grass

incubate keep eggs warm so the babies inside can grow

male animal that can become a father when it grows up. Men and boys are male people.

mate when male and female animals produce young

moult when a snake's old skin comes off its body and is replaced with a new skin

predator animal that catches and eats other animals for food

prey animal that gets caught and eaten by other animals

rainforest forest of very tall trees in hot, sunny, wet places

scales small hard pieces of skin on an animal's body that overlap like tiles on a roof

tropical word that describes a hot place with a long dry season and short wet season

venom spit containing poison

venomous able to make poison

Find out more

Books

Classifying Reptiles, Richard and Louise Spilsbury
   (Heinemann Library, 2003)

I Wonder Why Snakes Shed Their Skin and Other Questions About Reptiles,
   Amanda O'Neill (Kingfisher, 2002)

Keeping Unusual Pets: Snakes, Sonia Hernandes-Divers
   (Heinemann Library, 2003)

Rikki Tikki Tavi, Rudyard Kipling (Harper Collins, 2004)

Websites

There are some great king cobra pictures and pages of information at:
http://www.nationalgeographic.com/features/97/kingcobra/index-n.html

Get some more cobra facts at: http://www.cobras.org/report.htm

Disclaimer

Index

Asia 4, 6, 7, 26

camouflage 8

dry season 7, 18

eggs 20, 21, 22

fangs 16

grasslands 11

hunting 14, 15

mating 18, 19
mongooses 23
moulting 9, 22, 28

nests 20, 21

predators 24
prey 15, 16, 17, 23

rainforests 10, 26
rat snakes 15

scales 4, 13, 23
skin 4, 8, 9, 28

tropical 7, 8, 10, 11

venom 5, 16, 17, 23, 25, 27

wet season 7, 20, 22

Titles in the *Wild World* series include:

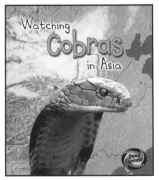

Hardback   0 431 19066 6

Hardback   0 431 19071 2

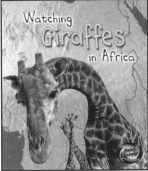

Hardback   0 431 19084 4

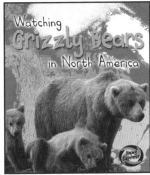

Hardback   0 431 19069 0

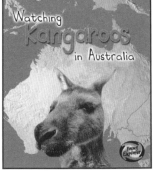

Hardback   0 431 19067 4

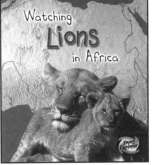

Hardback   0 431 19064 X

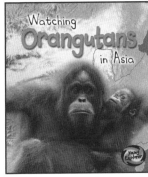

Hardback   0 431 19085 2

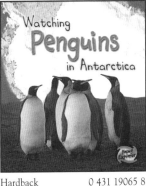

Hardback   0 431 19065 8

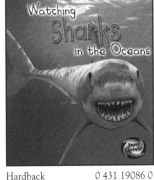

Hardback   0 431 19068 2

Hardback   0 431 19086 0

Hardback   0 431 19070 4

Find out about other Heinemann Library titles on our website www.heinemann.co.uk/library